German Shepherds

and Other Herding Dogs

Editorial:
Editor in Chief: Paul A. Kobasa
Project Manager: Cassie Mayer
Senior Editor: Christine Sullivan
Writer: Karen Ingebretsen
Researcher: Cheryl Graham
Manager, Contracts & Compliance
 (Rights & Permissions): Loranne K. Shields
Indexer: David Pofelski

Graphics and Design:
Manager: Tom Evans
Coordinator, Design Development
 and Production: Brenda B. Tropinski
Senior Designer: Don DiSante
Photographs Editor: Kathy Creech
Cartographer: John Rejba

Pre-Press and Manufacturing:
Director: Carma Fazio
Manufacturing Manager:
 Steven K. Hueppchen
Production/Technology Manager:
 Anne Fritzinger

For information about other World Book publications, visit our Web site at http://www.worldbookonline.com or call 1-800-WORLDBK (967-5325).

For information about sales to schools and libraries, call 1-800-975-3250 (United States), or 1-800-837-5365 (Canada).

World Book, Inc.
233 N. Michigan Avenue
Chicago, IL 60601
U.S.A.

Library of Congress Cataloging-in-Publication Data

German shepherds and other herding dogs.
 p. cm. -- (World Book's animals of the world)
 Includes index.
 Summary: "An introduction to German shepherds and other herding dogs, presented in a highly illustrated, question-and-answer format. Features include fun facts, glossary, resource list, index, and scientific classification list"--Provided by publisher.
 ISBN 978-0-7166-1373-2
 1. Herding dogs--Juvenile literature. 2. German shepherd dog--Juvenile literature. I. World Book, Inc.
 SF428.6.G47 2010
 636.737'6--dc22
                                    2009020164

World Book's Animals of the World
Set 6: ISBN: 978-0-7166-1365-7
Printed in China by Leo Paper Products LTD., Heshan, Guangdong
1st printing November 2009

Picture Acknowledgments: Cover: © cynoclub, Shutterstock; © Koljambus, Dreamstime; © Judy, Dreamstime; © Aleksey Ignatenko, Shutterstock; © Juniors Bildarchiv/Alamy Images.

© Christopher Appoldt, age fotostock 27; © Angela Hampton Picture Library/Alamy Images 15; © Bill Bachman, Alamy Images 31; © Fabrice Bettex, Alamy Images 4, 55; © Corbis Premium RF/Alamy Images 41; © Juniors Bildarchiv/Alamy Images 17, 51; © Fred Lord, Alamy Images 9; © Ovia Images/Alamy Images 29; AP Images 53; © Richard Hutchings, Corbis 59; Dreamstime 5, 7, 19, 35, 43, 47; © Victoria Yee, Image Bank/Getty Images 61; © istockphoto 21; © Corbis/SuperStock; © Photosindia/SuperStock 25; © Shutterstock 3, 5, 33, 37, 39, 45, 49, 57.

Illustrations: WORLD BOOK illustration by Roberta Polfus 13.

World Book's Animals of the World

German Shepherds

and Other Herding Dogs

WORLD
BOOK

a Scott Fetzer company
Chicago
www.worldbookonline.com

Contents

What Is a Herding Dog?

A herding dog is a breed of dog that was originally developed to keep livestock from straying and to help move them from one place to another. Herding dogs come in all sizes and shapes. They range from the short, sturdy Cardigan Welsh corgi *(KAWR gee)* to the tall, elegant Belgian shepherd. Some herding dogs have smooth coats; others have shaggy or wiry coats. Some are working dogs, while others are pets.

Herding dogs live in many parts of the world. Some breeds can be traced back hundreds of years. For example, the Beauceron *(boh suh rohn),* a French herding dog, dates back to 1587.

The American Kennel Club and the Canadian Kennel Club include these and many other breeds of dogs in the herding group. However, the Australian National Kennel Council includes these breeds in the working dog group, while the Kennel Club in the United Kingdom places these breeds in the pastoral group.

A German shepherd

How Did Breeds of Herding Dogs Develop?

Dogs and people have lived together for at least 14,000 years. We know little about the earliest history of dogs. It is thought that some ancient dogs helped people hunt, while others acted as guardians or companions.

As people's needs changed over time, they developed different breeds of dogs to meet those needs. (A breed is a group of animals that have the same type of ancestors.) Some dogs were bred to be hunting dogs. Others were bred to protect our homes. Still others were bred to be pets.

As farming became more important, people bred herding dogs to help with their cattle, sheep, goats, and the other animals they raised. Herding dogs were bred in a variety of shapes and sizes to do different jobs in different conditions. For example, Cardigan Welsh corgis are small dogs with short legs that originally drove cattle by nipping at their heels. Their small size helped them avoid the flailing hooves of these animals.

A border collie herding sheep

When and Where Did the German Shepherd Breed First Appear?

The German shepherd dog is a fairly new breed. It began with a large, wolflike dog that worked as a sheepherder in Germany during the late 1800's. In 1899, the dog was entered into a dog show, where a man named Max von Stephanitz *(shteh FAHN itz)* spotted it. Impressed with the qualities of this large, athletic dog, von Stephanitz purchased the dog and named him Horand von Grafrath *(GRAHF raht)*. Von Grafrath became the first registered German shepherd dog in 1899. Von Stephanitz also founded a club for German shepherd dogs in Germany. This club, which has branches in many countries, is now the largest individual breed club in the world.

In 1906, a dog named Mira von Offingen became the first German shepherd imported to the United States. In 1908, a German shepherd named Queen of Switzerland was the first of her breed to be officially registered by the American Kennel Club.

Map showing Germany, the country where the German shepherd dog developed

North
America

Asia

Germany

Atlantic
Ocean

Europe

Africa

Equator

Max von Stephanitz and his
dog, Horand von Grafrath

What Does a German Shepherd Look Like?

A German shepherd stands about 24 inches (61 centimeters) high at the shoulder. Its shape is somewhat like a wolf's. It has a long, wedge-shaped muzzle and pointed ears that stand up straight when the dog is alert.

A German shepherd has almond-shaped eyes that are usually a dark color. It has a long, bushy tail.

German shepherds have a double coat of hair. The longer outer hairs, known as guard hairs, help protect the dog from rain and snow. The fine hair of the undercoat helps to keep the dog warm. There are three varieties of German shepherds: rough-coated, long rough-coated, and long-haired.

German shepherds vary in color from black and tan to light brown. Some are all black or all white.

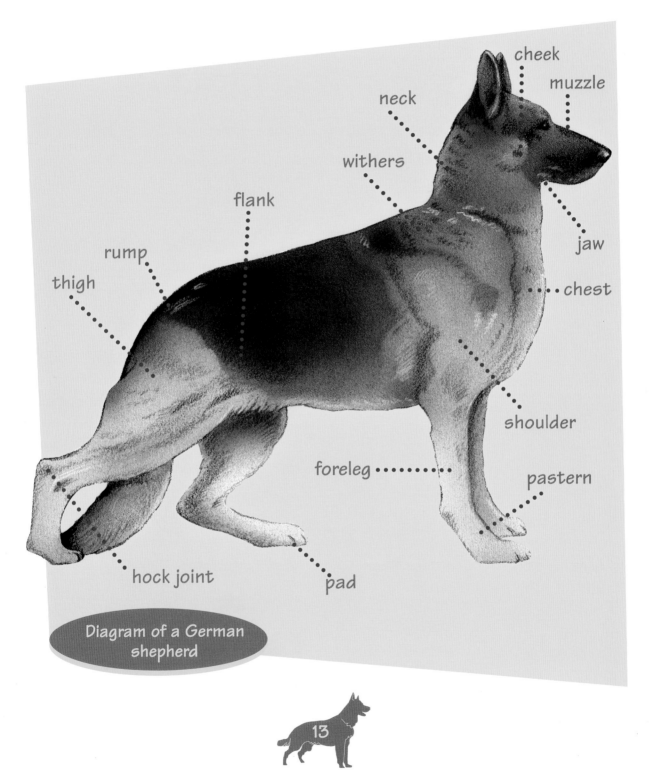

cheek

muzzle

neck

withers

jaw

flank

chest

rump

thigh

shoulder

foreleg

pastern

hock joint

pad

Diagram of a German
shepherd

What Kind of Personality Might a German Shepherd Have?

Every dog has its own personality, just as every person does. But some things tend to be true for most German shepherds. They are known for being fearless, self-confident, and very intelligent.

German shepherds are loyal and protective of their owners. They bark at any strangers who come to the home. They "guard" their family the same way they would guard livestock. They are not overly friendly when they meet new people, but they are very loving with their human families.

Most German shepherds have a lot of energy. They love to play. Because they were bred to be working dogs, they are often happiest when they have something to do, such as learning a new command, retrieving a plastic disk, or going for a run with their owner.

14

German shepherds are lovable family pets.

Is a German Shepherd the Dog for You?

German shepherds are great family dogs. They are smart, easy to train, and dedicated to their owners. They are patient and gentle with the children in the household. If you want a dog that will be part of the family, a German shepherd is a good choice. But if you plan to have the dog live outside, this may not be the breed for you. German shepherds do not do well left alone all the time.

Also remember that German shepherds are large dogs. They need a lot of daily exercise to keep both their minds and their bodies healthy. They also need more food than a smaller breed, and more space indoors and outdoors.

One more thing: German shepherds shed—a lot. The hair that looks so good on the dog doesn't look as good on your carpet. Be prepared for lots of grooming and vacuuming!

German shepherds love to go for walks.

What Should You Look for When Choosing a German Shepherd Puppy?

All puppies are cute, and you may be tempted to pick the first one you see. But it's important to choose carefully—you will have this dog for a dozen or more years. If possible, you should visit several litters before you decide.

When you visit a litter, look for an alert, confident puppy. Avoid the extremes—you don't want a shy, fearful puppy or an overly aggressive one.

The puppy's coat should be clean and glossy. Its eyes should be free of discharge (goopy stuff), and its ears should be clean.

If you want a pedigreed dog that you can breed or enter in shows, there are other things to consider. Your local library can help you find more information on choosing a pedigreed puppy. You can also visit the Web sites listed on page 64 for more information.

German shepherd
puppies

Should You Get an Older German Shepherd Instead of a Puppy?

Puppies are a lot of fun, but they are a lot of work, too. They need to be housebroken (taught where to go to the bathroom). They must be fed often, and they cannot be left alone for more than a few hours at a time. They are often very energetic and need a lot of attention. Also, no matter how carefully you select your puppy, you cannot be positive what its adult personality will be like.

Many adult German shepherds don't require the same high level of attention and care as a puppy. They are often calmer, and they may have already had obedience training. However, it will take some time for an older German shepherd to adjust to a new home, family, and routines. Be prepared to be patient for the first few months as your dog gets to know you. Soon you will have a devoted new member of your family.

An older German
shepherd

Should You Consider a Rescue German Shepherd?

A rescue dog is a dog that has been rescued from a shelter or owner that could not keep it. There are many groups devoted to helping these dogs. Some specialize in German shepherds.

Most of these groups work hard to match dogs with the best owners. The groups also make sure a dog is healthy, current on its shots, and is spayed or neutered before it goes to a new home. Most of these dogs are also housebroken. Some are crate-trained (trained to rest and sleep in their crate). Almost all have spent time with foster families learning basic commands and brushing up on their household "manners."

Many rescue German shepherds have found new homes. It's a partnership where everyone wins—the adopter gets a great companion, and the dog gets a great new home.

Giving a rescue German shepherd a new home can be rewarding for you and your new pet.

What Does a German Shepherd Eat?

German shepherds can be picky eaters. Luckily, dog food companies make a wide variety of products, so there's something for every dog at every stage of life. Your veterinarian can suggest the right type of food for your dog.

Some people feed their German shepherds table scraps. However, commercial dog food is a better source of the vitamins, minerals, and other things a dog needs to stay healthy. It's okay to give your German shepherd dog biscuits and other treats from time to time. Treats can be high in calories, though, so don't give them too often.

Chocolate contains a substance that is poisonous to dogs. Never give your dog chocolate. Other foods are bad for dogs too, including grapes and raisins, soft drinks, and sugarless candies.

Remember to make sure your dog always has plenty of fresh water.

A German shepherd
eating

Where Should a German Shepherd Sleep?

A German shepherd needs a dry, draft-free spot to sleep in and to retreat to when it wants to be alone. A kennel crate will serve this purpose. Be sure to get a crate large enough to comfortably hold the dog when it is fully grown.

You can also buy a dog bed at a pet store. Dog beds come in many shapes and materials. Any bedding must be washable to help protect your dog from fleas. You might want to put the dog bed in your bedroom, if you have space for it. Your dog would enjoy sleeping near you.

A German shepherd puppy may even want to sleep with you, on your bed. But remember, this "little" puppy is one day going to weigh 75 to 95 pounds (34 to 43 kilograms) and will take up much more of your bed! Think about that before you allow a habit that will be hard to break later.

A German shepherd on its bed

How Do You Groom a German Shepherd?

It's absolutely necessary to brush and comb a German shepherd regularly. Once or twice a week is enough most of the year, but during shedding season (spring and fall), you may need to do this every day. Your dog will need a bath a few times a year, and any other time it gets into a smelly or sticky substance.

You will need to clean a German shepherd's ears monthly. Pet stores sell a special cleaning product for this.

Your dog's nails must be trimmed when needed. Check them once a week, and if they need trimming, use pet nail clippers specially made for this purpose. You must be very careful not to cut the nails too short or it will hurt your dog. It is best to ask an adult to perform this task or to help you.

Your German shepherd's teeth must be brushed at least once a week. Pet stores sell special toothpaste and toothbrushes for dogs.

German shepherds need much grooming.

What About Training a German Shepherd?

Beyond housebreaking, a German shepherd needs obedience training. Even puppies can learn the basics in an obedience class. Dog trainers, veterinarians, and community groups offer obedience classes. You can also find out about classes at some pet stores. Check your local library for books and videos about training, too.

Training your dog will help it to learn how to behave and how to communicate. It is very important that you begin training your dog when it is a puppy so it does not form bad habits. Because they are smart and bred to follow commands, German shepherds are usually easy to train. They can even learn tricks!

Dog shows offer a chance for your German shepherd to compete in a number of special events. These include tracking, herding, agility, and a team sport called flyball, which is a relay race. You may want to train your dog in one of these activities, either for competition or just for fun.

German shepherds love
to learn new tricks.

31

What Kinds of Exercise or Play Are Needed?

German shepherds need a lot of daily exercise. It is not enough for them just to run around outside in a fenced yard. They need to go on long walks or runs with you, or run alongside you as you ride a bike. Fetching a ball or plastic flying disk is fun and good exercise, too.

It's just as important for a German shepherd to exercise its mind. This breed of dogs was designed to work, and they need challenges so they don't get bored. You can teach your dog to find family members by name or to find objects that you hide. You can teach it to fetch items or carry light objects. The more active your German shepherd is, the happier it will be.

German shepherds are
athletic dogs.

Do German Shepherds Like Water?

Most German shepherds love water. They are happy to swim in a lake or pond or even splash around in a small wading pool in a backyard. Some will just walk into the water up to their bellies and stand there. Others are ready to fetch any toy you throw into the water. Swimming is a great way for you and your dog to exercise when it's too hot to run or bike on dry land.

Some German shepherds, however, are afraid of water. If you have a puppy and you want it to grow up liking the water, start getting it used to the water as soon as possible.

If your family has an in-ground swimming pool, introduce your dog to the swimming pool as soon as possible. Even dogs that know how to swim may have trouble finding their way out of a pool if they accidentally fall in. Make sure the dog knows how to get out of the pool safely. Keep the pool area lit at night.

A German shepherd
playing fetch

35

Should You Breed Your German Shepherd?

There are many pets in the world that don't have homes. Because of this, most people should not breed their dogs, however fun it sounds to have cute puppies around.

Owners have a responsibility to keep their dogs from having unplanned puppies. A veterinarian can perform an operation so that your dog will not be able to produce puppies. Spaying prevents pregnancy in a female dog, and neutering makes a male dog permanently unable to father pups.

If you decide to breed your German shepherd dog, you will need to know how to care for the puppies. Have someone present who is experienced with dog births. Talk to your veterinarian about puppy foods and feeding methods.

A mother German shepherd and her young

Are There Special Organizations for German Shepherd Owners?

Yes. The German Shepherd Dog Club of America is one of the largest breed clubs in the United States. It works to promote the breed and support owners and their dogs. The club sponsors annual dog shows and performance trials. It has a juniors' program for those under age 18.

Another organization is the German Shepherd Dog Club of America-Working Dog Association. This group places a special focus on the working aspect of German shepherds, including herding, tracking, obedience, and protection. Member clubs sponsor surveys and host dog shows and competitions.

The German Shepherd Dog Club of Canada is that country's oldest active breed club. Dedicated to breed improvement, it has member organizations from coast to coast.

Australia also has several regional German Shepherd dog clubs.

Dog clubs may hold special gatherings for owners and their pets.

How Do German Shepherds Help People?

German shepherds often serve as police dogs. They can be trained to find drugs, bombs, and materials used to set fires illegally.

German shepherds have helped the armed forces in wartime. Among other things, they have worked as sentries (guards), messengers, and ambulance dogs that search for wounded or dead soldiers.

German shepherds were among the first guide dogs for the blind, and many perform this duty today. Others help people with hearing impairments or other physical challenges. Many German shepherds are also trained as therapy dogs, visiting people in hospitals and nursing homes.

Because of their excellent tracking and scenting ability, German shepherds also serve as search and rescue dogs. They can find people lost after an earthquake, avalanche, or other disaster, even in severe weather and rough conditions.

German shepherds are often used as rescue dogs.

What Are Some Other Herding Dog Breeds?

The American Kennel Club (AKC) sets the standards (accepted rules) for dog breeds in the United States and keeps track of pedigrees. It divides dog breeds into groups. The AKC's herding dog group includes many breeds, including the Australian cattle dog, Australian shepherd, collie, Canaan dog, Cardigan Welsh corgi, Pembroke Welsh corgi, puli *(POO lee)*, and Old English sheepdog, among others.

Groups similar to the AKC exist in Australia, Canada, and the United Kingdom. These organizations group breeds differently. The Canadian Kennel Club (CKC) has much the same grouping for herding dogs, except that it places the Canaan dog with the working group. The Kennel Club (KC), the United Kingdom's purebred organization, splits herding dogs between the pastoral group, the utility group, and the working group. The Australian National Kennel Council (ANKC) places all of the dogs listed above into the working-dog group, except for the Canaan dog, which it places in the nonsporting group.

A border collie

43

What Is a Collie?

A collie is a breed of dog that originated in Scotland, probably during the 1600's. Scottish farmers used collies to herd and guard flocks of sheep. British colonists brought collies to America during the 1700's. The breed became more popular after Queen Victoria of England brought several collies to Windsor Castle as pets in the 1860's.

There are two types of collies: the smooth collie and the rough collie. The smooth collie has a coarse, long-haired coat. The rough collie has a dense short-haired coat. Rough collies are rare outside of the United Kingdom. A collie may be brown and white; black, white, and tan; blue-gray; or all white.

Perhaps the most famous collie ever was the fictional character Lassie. This dog, a loyal and highly intelligent family pet, has been the subject of many stories, books, movies, and television series from 1938 to the present.

A collie

What Is an Old English Sheepdog?

An Old English sheepdog is a breed of dog that was developed in southwestern England in the late 1700's. The dogs were originally bred to herd sheep and cattle and help drovers (people who drove livestock to markets in cities).

Old English sheepdogs are large, strong, compact dogs. Most Old English sheepdogs are gray or blue, often with white markings, or mostly white with gray or blue markings. Their hair hangs down over their eyes. They have "bobbed" tails. They have an odd, shuffling way of walking, something like the way a bear walks.

Today, some Old English sheepdogs are still used as working dogs, but many others are pets. They are intelligent and friendly, and are good with children and other animals.

An Old English sheepdog

What Is a Cardigan Welsh Corgi?

A Cardigan Welsh corgi is a small, strong breed of dog that was first raised in Cardiganshire, Wales. Since about A.D. 1000, Cardigans have been used to herd cattle, nipping the feet of the cattle to drive them. Cardigans are related to dachshunds *(DAHKS hunds)*, small hound dogs that are commonly called "hot dogs" because of their long, narrow bodies.

The Cardigan Welsh corgi is a long, low dog. It looks a bit like a fox, with large ears and a long, bushy tail. Its short, rough coat may be almost any color or combination of colors, usually with white markings.

The name *corgi* comes from two Welsh words meaning "dwarf dog." And compared to other herding dogs, the Cardigan is small. But this small dog has a big heart: it is brave, loyal, and affectionate, and a good family pet.

48

A Cardigan Welsh corgi

What Is a Puli?

A puli is medium-sized herding dog that is known for its distinctive coat of fur. It is an ancient breed of dog that originated in Hungary. Shepherds have used the puli to help herd sheep for more than 1,000 years.

The puli has an unusual coat. If allowed to develop naturally, the coat forms ropelike cords in the adult dog. The cords can reach all the way to the ground. They give the dog a shaggy, moplike appearance. The dog's ears and eyes are covered, and you might wonder how it can see. The puli's coat can be black, rust-colored, gray, or white.

The puli is still used as a working dog, but many people keep it as a pet, too. It is an affectionate, playful dog that is also a good watchdog.

A puli

What Is a Dog Show Like?

Dog shows range from informal local events to national competitions sponsored by such groups as the Westminster Kennel Club. At most shows, purebred dogs are judged on their physical appearance. These shows are known as conformation competitions.

At all-breed shows, dogs from each breed are judged against a breed standard (an official description of the breed). Then the first-place dog from each breed in a group (for example, the herding dog group) competes for the title of Best of Group. After that, the first-place dogs from all the groups compete for the title of Best in Show.

German shepherds are judged on their physical appearance and their temperament. Ideal German shepherds are strong, muscular animals. They are expected to appear fearless and confident but not mean.

Even if you are not competing with your dog in a show, you can attend to watch the show. Several of the largest dog shows are shown on television each year.

This German shepherd dog won best in show.

Are There Dangers to Dogs Around the Home?

Even the smartest dogs can get into trouble around the home. Be sure to make your home as safe as possible for your dog. Here are a few things to look out for:

- Some plants are poisonous to dogs if eaten. If you have both houseplants and pets, ask your vet if the plants are safe to keep.

- Some dogs can open cabinet doors. If your dog can do this, either install childproof locks or make sure there are no household cleaners or chemicals in any cabinets your dog can reach. These items are often poisonous.

- Keep any mouse or insect bait or traps away from your dog. Store all prescription and over-the-counter drugs out of your dog's reach.

- If you have any windows open, be sure they are not open wide enough for your dog to jump through. An excited dog may jump out the window before you have a chance to stop it.

A German shepherd
at home

What Are Some Common Signs of Illness?

One common health problem in German shepherds is hip or elbow dysplasia *(dihs PLAY zhuh)*. Dysplasia refers to poor development of the hip or elbow. Signs of hip or elbow dysplasia can include difficulty when walking or running. Dogs with hip or elbow dysplasia may have an operation to fix the problem, or they may be treated with special vitamins.

Common signs of illness in all dogs include a change in behavior, a change in appetite, and fever. A dog that is ill or injured may be less active and may refuse to eat or may eat less. (Some illnesses, however, can cause a dog to eat or drink more.)

Other signs of illness can include vomiting and diarrhea, a dry nose, a dull coat, bald patches, unusual discharge from a dog's nose, ears, or eyes, and redness of the eyes.

Any time you suspect your dog might be ill, it's best to check with your vet promptly.

A tired German shepherd

57

What Routine Veterinary Care Is Needed?

Just like people, dogs need regular medical checkups to stay healthy and happy. Before you bring your German shepherd home, be sure to find a veterinarian you trust with your dog's health and well-being.

Puppies need a series of vaccinations (shots) to protect them from diseases. A new puppy needs a checkup when it is first adopted, and healthy adult dogs need an exam once a year. At the annual exam, the vet will bring the dog's vaccinations up to date. This is also a chance for you to discuss any training or behavioral questions and for the vet to tell you about new procedures and products.

Many vets recommend treating all puppies for parasitic worms until the puppies are three to four months old. Dogs in mosquito-infested areas should be given medicine the year around to prevent heartworms. A dog's annual checkup should include exams for heartworm and other worms.

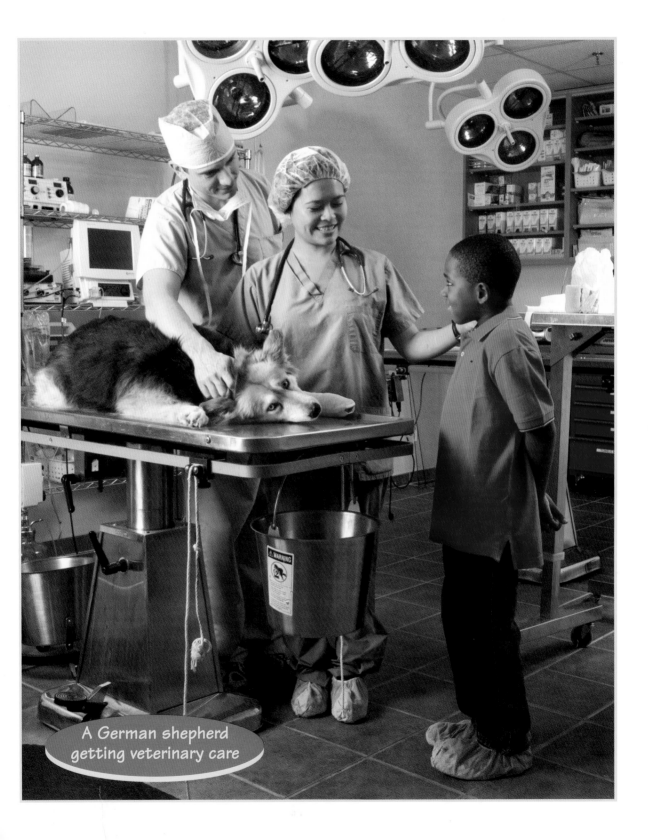

A German shepherd
getting veterinary care

What Are Your Responsibilities as an Owner?

Your first responsibility as an owner is to provide a healthy, loving home for your dog. This includes giving your dog proper medical care, plenty of exercise, and a healthy diet.

Being a responsible owner also means being considerate of others. You must keep your dog on a leash outdoors in public places unless you're in a specific area where you're allowed to let your dog go off-leash. You must also clean up after your dog when it has a bowel movement.

It is your responsibility to make sure that your dog doesn't bark so much that it disturbs other people. Many communities have laws about what they consider too much noise, including loud dogs.

Most importantly, be patient and loving with your dog. Remember, your dog is dependent on you for everything. It will reward you for your love and care by being your loyal companion.

Owning a dog can bring you much joy.

Herding Dog Fun Facts

→ A German shepherd named Rin Tin Tin starred in 27 movies and more than 150 television stories. At the height of his career, Rin Tin Tin received 10,000 fan letters a week.

→ The Briard, a very old breed of herding dog, appears in French tapestries dating as far back as the A.D. 700's.

→ Just two Pyrenean shepherds can manage a flock of 1,000 sheep.

→ According to legend, the Swedish vallhund was the Vikings' herding dog.

→ The first seeing eye dog in the United States was Buddy, a German shepherd. Her success inspired the guide dog program in the United States.

→ Many U.S. presidents have owned herding dogs, including Calvin Coolidge (Calamity Jane, a Shetland sheepdog, plus several collies), Franklin Delano Roosevelt (Major, a German shepherd, and Tiny, an Old English sheepdog), John F. Kennedy (Clipper, a German shepherd), Lyndon B. Johnson (Blanco, a white collie), and Ronald Reagan (Lucky, a bouvier des Flandres).

Glossary

ancestor An animal from which another animal is directly descended. Usually, *ancestor* is used to refer to an animal more removed than a parent or grandparent.

breed To produce animals by carefully selecting and mating them for certain traits. Also, a group of animals having the same type of ancestors.

breeder A person who breeds animals.

groom To take care of an animal, for example, by combing, brushing, or trimming its coat.

guard hairs The long, coarse hairs in the fur of an animal.

heartworm A worm that infests the hearts and arteries of dogs.

litter The young animals produced by an animal at one birthing.

livestock Farm animals; animals raised for their working ability or for their value as a source of food and other products.

neuter To operate on a male animal to make it unable to produce young.

parasite An organism (living creature) that feeds on and lives on or in the body of another organism, often causing harm to the being on which it feeds.

pedigree A record of an animal's ancestors.

purebred An animal whose parents are known to have both belonged to one breed.

shed To throw off or lose hair, skin, fur, or other body covering.

spay To operate on a female animal to make it unable to have young.

trait A feature or characteristic particular to an animal or breed of animals.

63

Index <small>(**Boldface** indicates a photo, map, or illustration.)</small>

For more information about German shepherds and other herding dogs, try these resources:

Books:

The Complete Dog Book for Kids by the American Kennel Club (Howell Book House, 1996)

German Shepherds by Mari C. Schuh (Bellwether Media, 2009)

Superpuppy: How to Choose, Raise, and Train the Best Possible Dog for You by Jill and Daniel Manus Pinkwater (Clarion Books, 2002)

Web sites:

American Kennel Club
http://www.akc.org

Australian National Kennel Council
http://www.ankc.org.au/

The Canadian Kennel Club
http://www.ckc.ca/en/

Humane Society of the United States
http://www.hsus.org

The Kennel Club
http://www.thekennelclub.org.uk/

German Shepherd Dog Club of America
http://www.gsdca.org/

German Shepherd Dog Club of Canada
http://www.gsdcc.ca/

German Shepherd Dog Council of Australia
http://www.gsdcouncilaustralia.org

German Shepherd Dog League of Great Britain
http://www.gsdleague.co.uk

Dog Classification

Scientists classify animals by placing them into groups. The animal kingdom is a group that contains all the world's animals. Phylum, class, order, and family are smaller groups. Each phylum contains many classes. A class contains orders, an order contains families, and a family contains genuses. One or more species belong to each genus. Each species has its own scientific name. Here is how the animals in this book fit into this system.

Animals with backbones and their relatives (Phylum Chordata)
Mammals (Class Mammalia)
Carnivores (Order Carnivora)

Dogs and their relatives (Family Canidae)

Domestic dog .... *Canis familiaris*